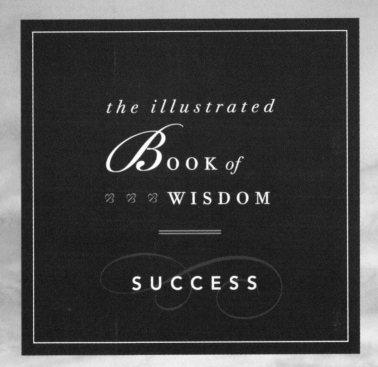

the illustrated

Book of

ƐƐƐ WISDOM

SUCCESS

SILVERLEAF
PRESS

The height of a man's success is gauged by his self-mastery, the depth of his failure by his self-abandonment. There is no other limitation in either direction. And this law is the expression of eternal justice. He who cannot establish a dominion over himself will have no dominion over others, he who masters himself shall be king.

—HORACE GREELEY

We shall not flag or fail. We shall go on to the end. We shall fight in France, we shall fight on the seas and the oceans, we shall fight with growing confidence and growing strength in the air, we shall defend our island, whatever the cost may be. We shall fight on the beaches, we shall fight on the landing grounds, we shall fight in the fields and in the streets, we shall fight in the hills; we shall never surrender.

—Winston Churchill

Success

doesn't come to you...
you go to it.

—Marva Collins

If...

If you can keep your head when all about you
　　Are losing theirs and blaming it on you.
If you can trust yourself when all men doubt you,
　　But make allowance for their doubting too;
If you can wait and not be tired by waiting,
　　Or being lied about, don't deal in lies,
　　Or being hated, don't give way to hating,
　　And yet don't look to good, nor talk to wise:
If you can dream—and not make dreams your master,
If you can think—and not make thoughts your aim;
If you can meet with Triumph and Disaster
　　And treat those two impostors just the same;
If you can bear to hear the truth you've spoken
　　Twisted by knaves to make a trap for fools,
　　Or watch the things ou gave your life to, broken,
　　And stoop and build 'em up with worn-out tools:
If you can make one heap of all your winnings
　　And risk it all on one turn of pitch-and-toss,
　　And lose, and start again at your beginnings
　　And never breath a word about your loss;
If you can force your heart and nerve and sinew
　　To serve your turn long after they are gone,
　　And so hold on when there is nothing in you
　　Except the Will which says to them: "Hold on!"...
If you can fill the unforgiving minute
　　With sixty seconds' worth of distance run,
　　Yours is the Earth and everything that's in it,
　　And—which is more—you'll be a Man, my son!

—*Rudyard Kipling*

Never

measure the height

of a mountain, until you have reached the top.

Then you will see how low it was.

DAG HAMMARSKJOLD

MAN'S GREATNESS

CONSISTS IN HIS ABILITY

TO DO AND THE PROPER

APPLICATION OF HIS POWERS

TO THINGS NEEDED TO BE

DONE.

–Frederick Douglass

S O   M

...walk around with a meaningless life. They seem half-asleep, even when they're busy doing things they think are important. ✿ This is because they're chasing the wrong things. The way you get meaning into your life is to devote yourself to loving others, devote yourself to your community around you, and devote yourself to creating something that gives you purpose and meaning.

—MORRIE SCHWARTZ

To every *thing* there is a *season*, and a time to every
    purpose under the heaven:
A time to be born, and a time to die; a time to plant,
    and a time to pluck up that which is planted;
A time to kill, and a time to heal; a time to break down,
    and a time to build up;
A time to weep, and a time to laugh; a time to mourn,
    and a time to dance;
A time to cast away stones, and a time to gather stones
    together; a time to embrace, and a time to refrain
    from embracing;
A time to get, and a time to lose; a time to keep, and a
    time to cast away;
A time to rend, and a time to sew; a time to keep
    silence, and a time to speak;
A time to love, and a time to hate; a time of war, and a
    time of peace.

                                    —*Ecclesiastes 3: 1-8*

The history of free men
is written not by chance,
but by choice—their choice.

—DWIGHT D. EISENHOWER

The abundant life is a process
of eternally becoming. It is not fixed
and static, but of necessity is ever
changing. What might be abundant life
to the child would, if unchanged,
become progressively less abundant as
he matures. It is a state of being,
where constant adjustments are necessary; where one is ever preparing
for the changing conditions of tomorrow.

• • •

—HUGH B. BROWN

The *harder the conflict,*

the more glorious the triumph.

What we obtain too cheaply,

we esteem to lightly.

'Tis dearness only that

–Thomas Paine *gives everything its value.*

I BELIEVE

life is constantly testing us for our

level of commitment,

and life's greatest rewards are

reserved for those who demonstrate

a never-ending commitment

to act until they achieve.

This level of resolve can move

mountains, but it must be constant

and consistent.

As simplistic as this may sound,

it is still the common denominator separating

those who live their dreams

from those who live in regret.

—ANTHONY ROBBINS

THE MARVELOUS
RICHNESS OF
HUMAN EXPERIENCE
WOULD LOSE
SOMETHING
OF REWARDING JOY
IF THERE WERE
NO LIMITATIONS
TO OVERCOME.
THE HILLTOP HOUR
WOULD NOT
BE HALF
SO WONDERFUL
IF THERE WERE
NO DARK VALLEYS
TO TRAVERSE.

—Helen Keller

F inish each day and be done
with it. You have done
what you could. Some
blunders and
absurdities no doubt
crept in; forget
them as soon as you
can. Tomorrow
is a new day; begin
it well and serenely
and with
too high a spirit
to be encumbered with
your old nonsense.

—RALPH WALDO EMERSON

There are only two roads that lead to something like human happiness. They are marked by the words...love and achievement.... In order to be happy oneself it is necessary to make at least one other person happy.... The secret of human happiness is not in self-seeking but in self-forgetting.

–Dr. Theodor Reik

The world has many unsung heroes

*S*uccess is achievable without public recognition, and the world has many unsung heroes. The teacher who inspires you to pursue your eduation to your ultimate ability is a success. The parents who taught you the noblest human principles are a success…. The relatives, friends, and neighbors with whom you develop a reciprocal relationship of respect and support—they, too, are successes. The most menial workers can properly consider themselves successful if they perform their best and if the product of their work is of service to humanity.

 MICHAEL DEBAKEY

Do it

Do it right! Do it right now!

—*Anonymous*

The most successful men in the end are those whose success is the result of steady accretion.... It is the man who carefully advances step by step, with his mind becoming wider and wider–and progressively better able to grasp any theme or situation–persevering in what he knows to be practical, and concentrating his though upon it, who is bound to succeed in the greatest degree.

—Alexander Graham Bell

Imagine life as a game in which you are juggling five balls in the air. You name them—work, family, health, friends, and spirit—and you're keeping all of these in the air. You will soon understand that work is a rubber ball. If you drop it, it will bounce back. But the other four balls—family, health, friends, and sprit are made of glass. If you drop one of these, they will be irrevocably scuffed, marked, nicked, damaged, or even shattered. They will never be the same. you must understand that and strive for balance in your life.

— BRIAN DYSON

Only if you reach the boundary will the boundary recede before you. And if you don't, if you confine your efforts, the bounday will shrink to accommodate itself to your efforts. And you can only expand your capacities by working to the very limit.

— HUGH NIBLEY

YOUR BOUNDARIES...

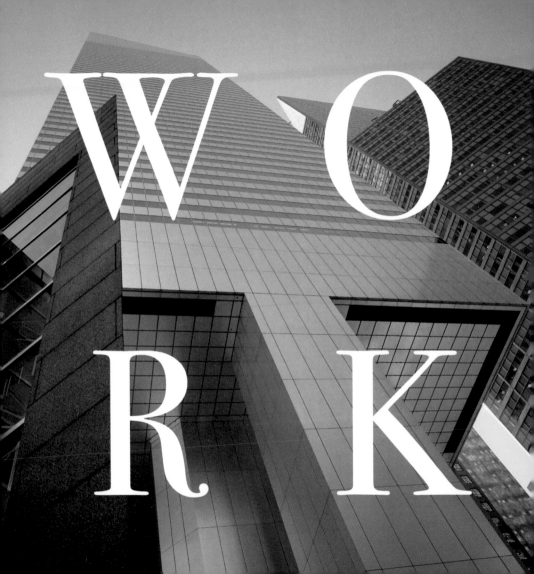

... BE AWARE, for the degree of your awareness will determine the measure of your aliveness. Some have eyes but see not, ears but hear not, and hearts that do not understand. No day will dawn for him who is asleep, and no dream will come true for him who only dreams ... the three rules for success are, WORK, WORK, WORK.

—*Hugh B. Brown*

H*e has achieved success who has lived well, laughed often, and loved much; who has gained the respect of intelligent men and the love of little children; who has filled his niche and accomplished his task, who has left the world better than he found it, whether by an improved poppy, a perfect poem, or a rescued soul; who has never lacked appreciation of earth's beauties, nor failed to express it; who has always looked for the best in others and given the best he had; whose life is an inspiration; whose memory a benediction.*

ROBERT LOUIS STEVENSON

YOU WILL BECOME AS SMALL

AS YOUR CONTROLLING DESIRE,

AS GREAT AS YOUR DOMINANT ASPIRATION.

:: James Allen

Imaginary obstacles

are insurmountable.

Real ones aren't.

Fear can create even more

imaginary obstacles

than ignorance can.

That's why the smallest

step away from

speculation and

into reality can be an

amazing relief.

The Reality Solution means:

Do it before you're ready.

Barbara Sher

DO IT BEFORE YOU'RE READY

No success

can compensate

for failure

in the home.

—Benjamin Disraeli

Success in the home…

A formula for success...

Would you like me to give you a formula for success?
It's quite simple, really. Double your rate of failure.
You are thinking of failure as the enemy of success.
But it isn't at all. You can be discouraged by failure
or you can learn from it. So go ahead and make mis-
takes. Make all you can. Because remember that's
where you will find success.

—Thomas J. Watson

I DO NOT THINK THERE IS ANY OTHE

UALITY SO ESSENTIAL   TO SUCCESS OF

ANY KIND AS THE

QUALITY OF

Perseverance.

IT OVERCOMES

ALMOST EVERY-

THING, EVEN

NATURE.

—JOHN D. ROCKEFELLER

The only limit to

our realization of

tomorrow will be

our doubts of today.

—FRANKLIN D. ROOSEVELT

THE PERSON WHO TRIES TO LIVE
ALONE WILL NOT SUCCEED AS A
HUMAN BEING. HIS HEART WITHERS IF
IT DOES NOT ANSWER ANOTHER HEART.
HIS MIND SHRINKS AWAY IF
HE HEARS ONLY THE ECHOES OF HIS OWN
THOUGHTS AND FINDS NO
OTHER INSPIRATION.

—Pearl S. Buck

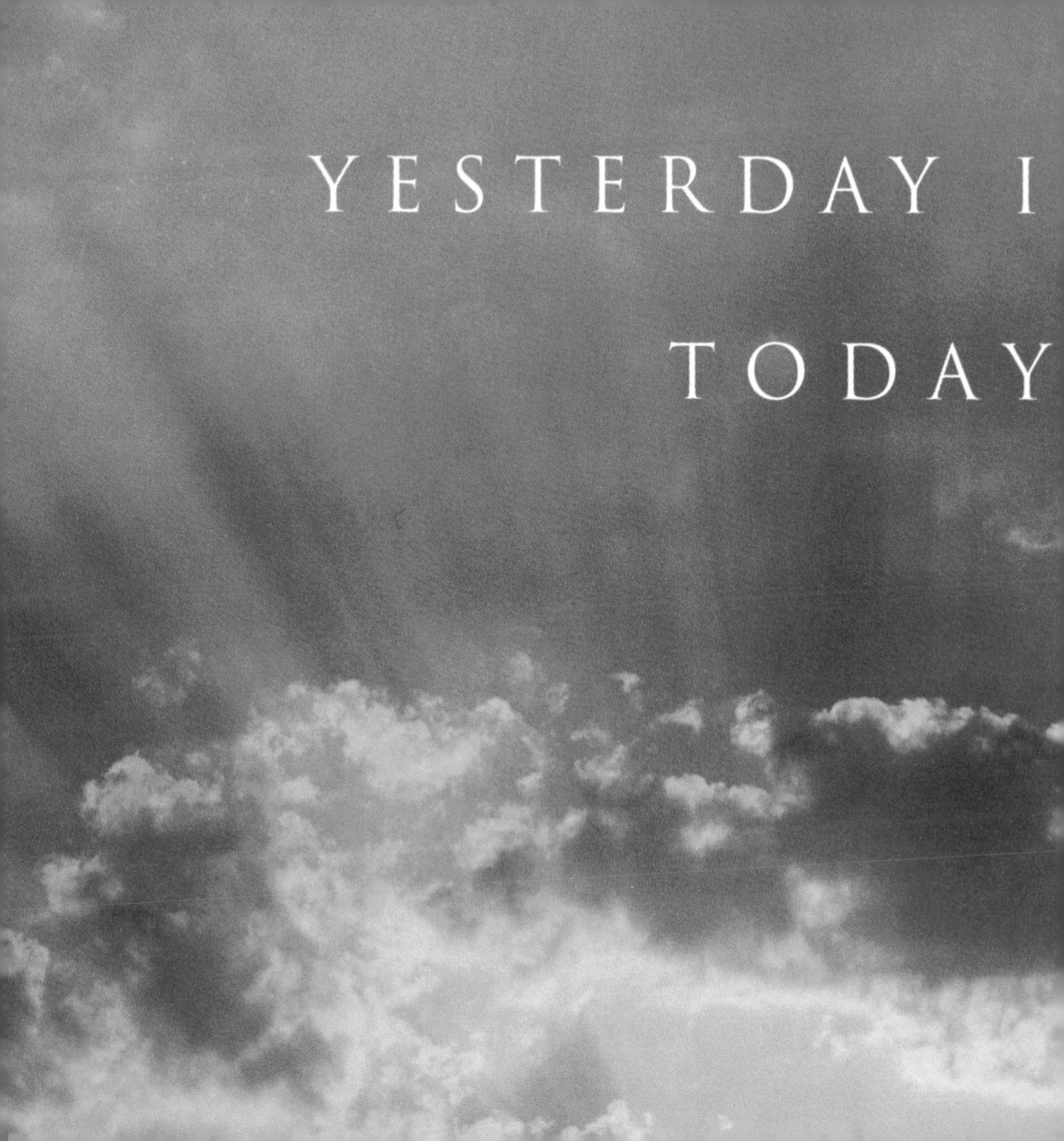
YESTERDAY I
TODAY

DARED TO STRUGGLE.

I DARE TO WIN.

—BERNADETTE DEVLIN

People

who have accomplished work worthwhile have had a very high sense of the way to do things. They have not been content with mediocrity. They have not confined themselves to the beaten tracks; they have never been satisfied to do things just as others do them, but always a little better. They always pushed things that came to their hands a little higher up, this little farther on, that counts in the quality of life's

work. It is constant effort to be first-class in everything one attempts that conquers the heights of excellence.

—Orison Swett Marden

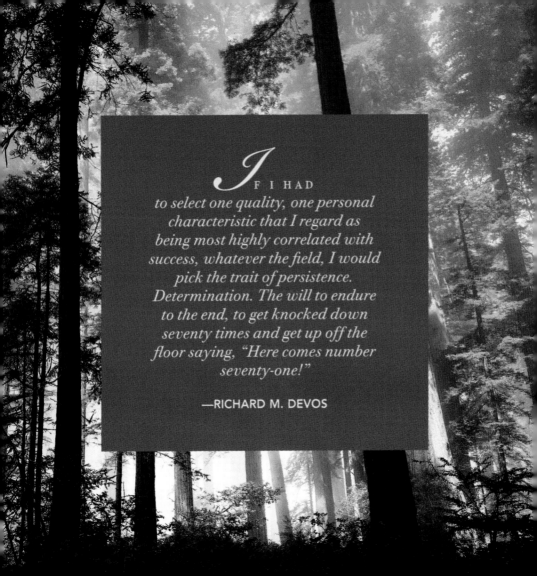

*I*F I HAD to select one quality, one personal characteristic that I regard as being most highly correlated with success, whatever the field, I would pick the trait of persistence. Determination. The will to endure to the end, to get knocked down seventy times and get up off the floor saying, "Here comes number seventy-one!"

—RICHARD M. DEVOS

Our deepest fear is not that we are inadequate. Our

deepest fear is that we are powerful beyond measure. It is our light,

not our darkness that frightens us most... .

There is nothing enlightened about

shrinking so that people won't feel insecure around you. We were

born to make manifest the glory of God that is within us.

It's not just in some of us; it's in all of us. And when we let our own light

shine, we unconsciously give other people permission to do the same.

As we are liberated from our own fear, our presence

automatically liberates others.

— NELSON MANDELA

these

THEN ARE MY LAST WORDS TO YOU:
BE NOT AFRAID OF LIFE. BELIEVE THAT LIFE
IS WORTH LIVING AND YOUR BELIEF WILL
HELP CREATE THE FACT.

—WILLIAM JAMES

give **MORE** *than you receive*

Try not to become a man of success,
but rather to become a man of value.
He is considered successful in our day
who gets more out of life than he puts in.
But a man ov value
will give more than he receives.

ALBERT EINSTEIN

YOU CAN ONLY BECOME TRULY ACCOMPLISHED AT SOME-
THING YOU LOVE. DON'T MAKE MONEY YOUR GOAL. INSTEAD,
PURSUE THE THINGS YOU LOVE DOING, AND THEN DO THEM
SO WELL THAT PEOPLE CAN'T TAKE THEIR EYES OFF YOU.

—Maya Angelou

*Y*ou are not here merely to make a living. You are here in order to enable the world to live more-amply, with greater vision, with a finer spirit of hope and achievement. You are here to enrich the world, and you impoverish yourself if you forget the errand.

WOODROW WILSON

Existance is a strange bargain. Life owes us little; we owe it everything. The only true happiness comes from squandering ourselves for a purpose.

JOHN MASON BROWN

Success equals goals; all else is commentary

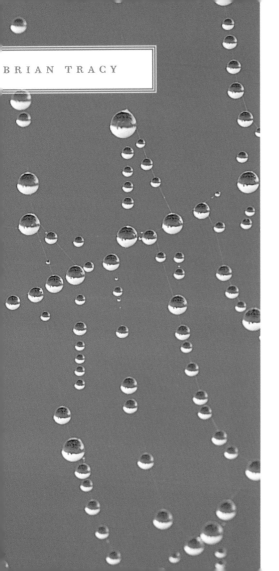

BRIAN TRACY

When I was younger, I thought that the key to success was just hard work. But the real foundation is faith. Faith—the idea that "I can do it"—is the opposite of fear ("What if I fail?"). And faith creates motivation which in turn leads to commitment, hard work, preparation...and eventually success.

—Howard Twilley

It is not ease

but effort,

not facility

but difficulty,

that makes

man....

...There is perhaps no station in life in which difficulties do not have to be encountered and overcome before any decided means of success can be achieved.

—*Samuel Smiles*

OVER

AND ABOVE

No student
ever attains very eminent
success by simply doing what is
required of him: it is the amount
and excellence of what is over
and above the required, that
determines the greatness
of ultimate distinction.

CHARLES KENDALL ADAMS

How far

YOU GO IN LIFE DEPENDS ON YOUR BEING
TENDER WITH THE YOUNG, COMPASSIONATE
WITH THE AGED, SYMPATHETIC WITH THE
STRIVING AND TOLERANT OF THE WEAK AND

STRONG. BECAUSE SOMEDAY
YOU WILL HAVE BEEN ALL
OF THESE.

GEORGE WASHINGTON CARVER

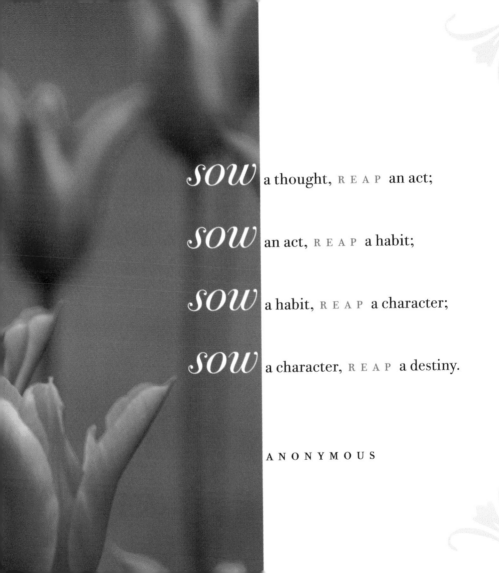

sow a thought, REAP an act;

sow an act, REAP a habit;

sow a habit, REAP a character;

sow a character, REAP a destiny.

ANONYMOUS

FOR TRUE SUCCESS, IT MATTERS WHAT OUR
GOALS ARE. AND IT MATTERS HOW WE GO
ABOUT ATTAINING THEM. THE MEANS ARE AS
IMPORTANT AS THE ENDS. HOW WE GET THERE
IS AS IMPORTANT AS WHERE WE GO.

—*Tom Morris*

 PERSISTENCE

Nothing in the world can take the place of persistence. Talent wil not; nothing is more common than unsuccessful men with talent. Genius will not; unrewarded genius is almost a proverb. Education will not; the world is full of educated derelicts. Persistence and determination alone are omnipotent. The slogan, "press on" has solved, and always will solve, the problems of the human race.

— CALVIN COOLIDGE

AND DETERMINATION

MY WILL...

...shall shape the future. Whether I fail or
succeed shall be no man's doing but my own. I am the force; I can
clear any obstacle before me or I can be lost
in the maze. My choice, my responsibility;
win or lose, only I hold the key to my destiny.

ELAIN MAXWELL

Aim for success, not perfection. Never give up your right to be wrong, because then you will lose the ability to learn new things and move forward with your life. Remember that fear always lurks behind perfectionism. Confronting your fears and allowing yourself the right to be human can, paradoxically, make yourself a happier and more productive person.

—DAVID M. BURNS

Whether you think that you can, or that you can't, you are usually right.

—HENRY FORD

IF I HAVE BEEN OF SERVICE,
IF I HAVE GLIMPSED MORE OF
THE NATURE AND ESSENCE
OF ULTIMATE GOOD,
IF I AM INSPIRED TO
REACH WIDER HORIZONS OF
THOUGHT AND ACTION, IF I
AM AT PEACE WITH MYSELF,
IT HAS BEEN A SUCCESSFUL DAY.

{ ALEX NOBLE }

I t is possible that the scrupulously honest man may not grow rich so fast as the unscrupulous and dishonest one; but the success will be of a truer kind, earned without fraud or injustice. And even though a man should for a time be unsuccessful, still he must be honest: better lose all and save character. For character is itself a fortune...

—*Samuel Smiles*

Life is succession of MOMENTS.

To live EACH ONE is to succeed.

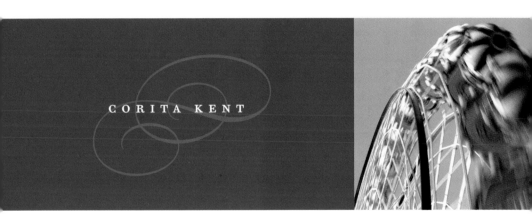

CORITA KENT

*S*OMEONE HAS
DEFINED GENIUS
AS INTENSITY
OF PURPOSE:
THE ABILITY TO DO,
THE PATIENCE TO
WAIT.... PUT THESE
TOGETHER AND YOU
HAVE GENIUS,
AND YOU HAVE
ACHIEVEMENT.

—Leo J. Muir

TO DO

AND TO WAIT

I long to accomplish a great and noble task, but it is my chief duty to accomplish humble tasks as though they were great and noble. The world is moved along, not only by the mighty shoves of its heroes, but also by the aggregate of the tiny pushes of each honest worker.

HELEN KELLER

EACH TINY push

T*he person who makes a success of living is*

the one who sees his goal steadily and aims for it unswervingly.

That is dedication..

IT IS THE

HEART THAT MAKES

A MAN RICH.

HENRY WARD BEECHER

Silverleaf Press books are available exclusively
through Independent Publishers Group.

For details write or telephone
Independent Publishers Group, 814 North Franklin Street,
Chicago, Illinois 60610; (312) 337-0747.

Silverleaf Press
8160 South Highland Drive
Sandy, 84093

ISBN 1-933317-40-X

Printed in Malaysia
1 2 3 4 5 6 7 8 9 10

Book design by David Eliason